MW01060063

Practical Martial Arts

F O R

SPECIAL FORCES

William Beaver

Paladin Press • Boulder, Colorado

For my wife, Suhair, and my son, Jacob.

Practical Martial Arts for Special Forces
by William Beaver

Copyright © 1996 by William Beaver
ISBN 0-87364-866-8
Printed in the United States of America

Published by Paladin Press, a division of
Paladin Enterprises, Inc., P.O. Box 1307,
Boulder, Colorado 80306, USA.
(303) 443-7250

Direct inquiries and/or orders to the above address.

Contents

Introduction   1

Chapter 1: Unarmed Fighting   11

Chapter 2: Ground Fighting   45

Chapter 3: Grab Counters   59

Chapter 4: Firearm and Knife Defense   65

Chapter 5: Mental Training   85

Appendix: Training Methods and Drills   91

About the Author   101

Acknowledgments

This book is the result of many people, some with very sensitive positions, allowing me to enter their world and draw on their knowledge. First and foremost, I thank my two barometers of reality: Matthew Young and James Watt.

From the martial arts field, appreciation must be extended to all the instructors who have shared a wealth of technique and information with me over the years. In particular, I must thank my own personal instructors Walter Andrae, Bob Maschmeier, Joe Halbuna, George Anderson, and Tom Sergeant. My late father's best friend, Sheriff Larry Overholt, has been my martial arts mentor and role model from the beginning. They don't come any finer.

In the special forces community, I am grateful for the assistance and friendship of operators like Richard Fike, Doc Rich, Joe Linza, Randy Curtiss, Mike Coker, Dave,

Will, Nick Nowatney, the members of the Green Felt Table, and all the other 5th Group team members who keep passing through. My door is always open, gentlemen.

Special thanks goes to the "elite troops" who volunteered for the most dangerous duty—my photography sessions: Ayman Al-Harmi, Julian Barnsley, and Masoud Al-Fuaid.

And finally, my gratitude knows no bounds for my family, friends, and the students of Kajukenbo of Kuwait, all of who put up with my occasional bouts of restlessness. I hope in the end you think it was worth it.

Preface

When I was editor of *Karate/Kung Fu Illustrated*, I conducted an informal survey, asking people around the United States to send me advertisements from the Yellow Pages or any other source in which people claimed to be instructors for the Special Forces, the Rangers, the SEALs, or other elite military/law enforcement units. I was completely shocked by the response, receiving countless letters containing ads where people claimed they had taught the U.S. Special Forces in Vietnam or some other remote place. Many more instructors advertised that they had secretly taught (pick any three letters) the CIA, FBI, DEA, or the DIA.

Research I had done for my magazine and my own personal military experience and contacts revealed that the vast majority of these claims were of course false. It seems that some instructors used the briefest contact with special forces personnel as a viable reason to advertise themselves as qualified special forces instructors.

In 1992, the year after the liberation of Kuwait from Iraq, the entire Kuwaiti military was being rebuilt. My marriage to the daughter of a former Kuwaiti ambassador brought me to Kuwait that same year. Through a chance introduction, I met the commander of the Kuwait Special Forces. He was interested in finding a martial arts instructor for his newly reformed unit, but he wanted to avoid the taekwon do and shotokan instructors in Kuwait. He felt that they concentrated too much on sports and competition, but more importantly, he didn't feel that the techniques worked well for the special forces soldier.

A 4th degree black belt in kajukenbo at the time, I had just opened the first full-time martial arts school in Kuwait. I had also met members of the American 5th Special Forces Group who were in country training the Kuwait Special Forces. The Americans asked me to teach them privately, which I did and have continued to do periodically. Having served a very short time in the 11th Special Forces Group myself, I was at least knowledgeable enough about the special operations community to adapt my street-oriented kajukenbo techniques to their particular needs.

The commander of the Kuwait Special Forces, after seeing a demonstration of my training methods and techniques, offered me a contract to teach his soldiers on a full-time basis. The contract was simple: I could train as many men as I wanted by any means I wanted, but I would have to get results.

I have trained in martial arts since 1978, and as a result of my editorial position at *Karate/Kung Fu Illustrated* and *Black Belt* magazines, I have also learned a great deal from some of the best martial artists in the world. I have spent the last few years trying specifically to refine and develop a means of teaching martial arts to special forces soldiers—elite troops with unique missions. *Practical Martial Arts for Special Forces* is the result of that experience.

Introduction

T he contemporary image of the special
forces soldier is a gross misconception
born mostly of film. As George Leonard
pointed out in his excellent article "The Warrior"
(*Esquire*, July 1986):

> America has discovered a new hero . . . he
> is an elite forces man with the body of a
> Western bodybuilder and the mindset of an
> Eastern martial artist. He is Chuck Norris
> in *Missing in Action* and *The Delta Force*,
> Arnold Schwarzenegger in *Commando*, and
> Fred Ward in *Remo Williams: The Adventure
> Begins*. Above all, he is Sylvester Stallone in
> *Rambo: First Blood, Part II*

Although the name "special forces" is found in

the army, there are also elite units in most other military branches and even some federal agencies. In 1987, Congress formally authorized the formation of the U.S. Special Operations Command. The term "special forces" now carries considerable baggage, usually meaning a soldier or perhaps federal agent whose mission and training are elite and highly specialized. Generally speaking, the media have added the larger, more mysterious cloak-and-dagger elements to the special forces.

As Leonard made clear in his article, and as any person who has worked with authentic special forces knows, these elite soldiers are, above all else, expert learners. They know what specific skills their mission requires them to master. This self-knowledge is where the foremost problem with teaching martial arts to special forces begins:

The majority of people trying to instruct elite troops in martial arts usually don't have an appreciation for their true needs. What usually happens is that a person is given the chance to teach the members of an elite unit but fails to adapt the training to their particular mission, mainly because he doesn't know what their mission is. Instead he draws the soldiers into his world of martial arts, utilizing some section of his skills that he thinks might work for them.

Although a martial arts instructor may be an excellent teacher, his training will entirely miss the point unless it specifically addresses the elite unit mission. For the past several years, I have been living and working in Kuwait, which has included teaching techniques from the kajukenbo system to the Kuwait Special Forces. Some of the soldiers I have trained have also been A-Team members from the American 5th Special Forces Group assigned to Kuwait. Through this experience, I was forced to radically alter my view of what works for special forces.

Introduction

WHAT ARE THE NEEDS OF
THE SPECIAL FORCES SOLDIER?

One of the first commando instructors to address this specific question was William Ewart Fairbairn, a British army officer who, with his partner Maj. William Sykes, invented the Fairbairn-Sykes double-edged fighting knife. Both had served for many years on the Shanghai Police before being recruited to train members of the Royal Commandos, as well as agents from the Office of Strategic Services (OSS) and Special Operations Executive (SOE) during World War II.

Fairbairn's training was remembered by U.S. Army Maj. Gen. John K. Singlaub in his memoirs, *Hazardous Duty* (New York: Summit Books, 1991):

> The Major's [Fairbairn's] fighting credo was simple: A well-trained man had nothing to fear from close combat. Rather, if this man was properly armed, all nearby adversaries had everything to fear. We would become so proficient with a variety of Allied and enemy weapons over the coming months, he promised, that using them would become instinctive.

Although in this case Fairbairn was talking about learning to use weapons, including his fighting knife, he also demanded proficiency in unarmed fighting skills. Why did Fairbairn consider martial arts training to be so important for special forces? Another of Fairbairn's students, George Langelaan, provides the answer in his classic book, now long out of print, about the Special Operations Executive, *No Colours or Crest* (London: Panther, 1961):

> [Fairbairn] gave us more and more self-confidence which gradually grew into a sense of

3

physical power and superiority that few men ever acquire. By the time we finished our training, I would have willingly enough tackled any man, whatever his strength, size, or ability. He taught us to face the possibility of a fight without the slightest tremor of apprehension, a state of mind which very few professional boxers ever enjoy and which so often means more than half the battle. Strange as this may seem, it is understandable when a man knows for certain that he can hurt, maul, injure, or even kill with the greatest of ease, and that during every split second of a fight, he has not one but a dozen different openings, different possibilities to choose from.

There are the reasons, simple and easy to understand. A special forces trooper faces personal combat with the clearest of alternatives: "Either he dies or I do."

SPECIAL FORCES REQUIREMENT ONE

One of the primary reasons, then, for training elite troops in martial arts is to give them a decided mental and physical edge. The techniques themselves will most likely not even be used. The modern elite soldier is heavily armed with a vast array of weapons specific to his mission. Sometimes he will engage the enemy only as a last alternative, especially if his mission is to gather intelligence without leaving any trace of having been there.

The special forces soldier will use martial arts only as a last resort, such as when all his other weapons fail, or during an escape and evasion attempt.

If martial arts are his weapon in a situation like trying to escape and evade, then the techniques taught

Soldiers who will be using martial arts to escape and evade will be hungry and near exhaustion.

to him must take into account his probable physical condition: hungry and nearing exhaustion. He cannot rely on techniques that require considerable strenuous activity. They must be quick, easy, and efficient.

SPECIAL FORCES REQUIREMENT TWO

Martial arts training for elite soldiers must be mission specific, which generally means causing debilitating injury or death. The soldier who will use martial arts in an escape and evasion situation, or whose other weapons have failed, will have no need for restraining techniques. If he must fight, he will not capture the enemy, he will kill him. Fairbairn addressed this issue in his excellent book *Get Tough: How to Win in Hand-To-Hand Fighting* (Boulder: Paladin Press, 1979):

> There are some who will be shocked by the methods advocated here. To them I say, "In war you cannot afford the luxury of squeamishness. Either you kill or capture, or you will be captured or killed. We've got to be tough to win, and we've got to be ruthless— tougher and more ruthless than our enemies."

Special forces soldiers will have no problem learning to kill because they've already mastered the most important aspect of combat: they do not personalize the enemy. They do not see faces. What they see, and what you must teach them to observe, is a target, or in the case of hand-to-hand combat, a collection of vital target points.

SPECIAL FORCES REQUIREMENT THREE

The training most likely will be given in a very

short period (often six weeks or less); therefore, the techniques must be limited and flexible. Once the instructor understands the mission of the soldier he is training, the techniques chosen can be tailored for maximum adaptability.

One example of how to limit techniques can be made through observation of the physical appearance of the men you train daily. Without exception, the men I train all wear very short hair, so we waste no time on techniques where the soldier's hair is grabbed.

I also choose techniques that can be used against more than one kind of attack (which are more fully discussed in Chapter 1). For example, the techniques for countering a common barroom round punch can also be used against someone using the same motion while swinging a club or pipe. The soldier doesn't memorize specific techniques but instead learns to react to general motions—the rounded motion, an overhead strike, and so on.

SPECIAL FORCES REQUIREMENT FOUR

The martial arts techniques chosen should require no changes to the body, such as significantly improved flexibility. You must start where the soldier already is. If you have only six weeks to train a group of soldiers, certain physical skills like rolling and falling will improve, but altering the body should not be a prerequisite for the skills to be learned. This means that techniques like high taekwon do kicks are inappropriate for the special forces soldier. (Please note that I said *high* taekwon do kicks, not taekwon do kicks in general.)

Although other instructors might say that improved flexibility will happen as a result of the training, maintaining skills with the techniques should not require maintaining the flexibility. The physical training demands placed on the special forces soldier may indeed include some flexibility work, but they often do not; therefore, his technique arsenal should not require it for effectiveness.

SPECIAL FORCES REQUIREMENT FIVE

Martial arts techniques must be maintained with a minimum of effort and time. The typical special forces soldier spends the majority of his time either keeping his own skills polished or teaching his skills to others. Consider the list of skills needed by special forces soldiers who were taught aikido by George Leonard ("The Warrior," *Esquire* 1986):

> They were Green Berets, members of the U.S. Army Special Forces, who had volunteered for an experimental six-month course in advanced mind-body training run by a Seattle-based organization called Sportsmind. Most of them had gone through Army Ranger training. All were skilled in hand-to-hand combat and the use of various weapons, parachuting, scuba diving, rock climbing, skiing, escape and evasion, and other specialized military skills, some of them classified. The experimental training program, designed to add a psychophysical component to an already rigorous schedule of military training, included daily aikido training aimed at integrating the physical and mental.

Even though the U.S. Army had provided the men with the Sportsmind program, their military skills, as the priority, still had to be kept fresh. Most special forces programs are the same, with martial arts training being only one small course in a buffet of skills taught. The techniques chosen must be ones that can be maintained without taking considerable amounts of time and are ideal if they can be included as part of the unit's regular physical training program.

• • •

This book covers the general areas of training through which I take the special forces soldier during a six-week training course lasting two hours each day. The soldier learns techniques in empty-hand fighting, ground fighting, grabs, gun and knife techniques, and improvised weapons. In order for a special forces soldier to learn these skills in such a short period of time, I also include a considerable number of drills for training in each area.

This book is not intended as a complete manual of martial arts techniques for special forces soldiers but rather as a means of classification—a way to help them learn and to aid the instructor of elite troops in choosing the most crucial techniques from any particular style. Given the general guidelines and strategies in this book, it follows that almost any martial arts style could, in theory, be adapted for special forces use.

In a street fight situation, protecting yourself requires a certain degree of attention to the law, since going too far can turn you into the defendant instead of the defender. Special forces soldiers generally do not concern themselves with such complexities. For them, the rules of war never change. Either the enemy dies or they do, and their best chance of staying alive begins with their training.

Unarmed Fighting

Perhaps you are a special forces soldier who wants to add the techniques of martial arts to your list of personal weapons, or maybe you're an instructor who will teach elite troops. You've been given six weeks or less to train a group of highly motivated men in martial arts techniques. Just imagine the possibilities.

Most people will immediately start listing all the situations a person might face, perhaps starting with a general heading like "Defending against . . ." and then listing such attacks as kicks, front holds, wrist holds, rear holds, front chokes, rear strangles, straight punches, round punches, knife attacks, club attacks, firearm attacks, improvised weapons, arm locks, wrist locks, multiple attackers, and knockdowns. Then, of course, other possible situations and environments are added: fighting in tight, confined places, fighting in groups, fighting from or around vehicles, fighting against a wall, fighting from sitting positions, and countless others.

Who could be expected to remember, let alone use and even more importantly master, such a complex list of techniques in such a short time? The hard choice to make is not what to leave in, it's what to leave out. Leaving anything out would at first seem to be martial arts heresy, unless, of course, a method of training exists that would allow someone to react to situations without being instructed in specific ways to handle each and every scenario. This book suggests just such a method.

The first thing to understand about training special forces soldiers in martial arts is that many of the traditional goals do not apply. A master might have his students spend countless minutes, class after class, squatting in a horse stance with the goal of developing strong legs and, more importantly, strong wills. Building tough minds and bodies will always be a solid objective of traditional martial arts training, but attempting the same while training elite troops is, to borrow a cliché, simply reinventing the wheel.

Nothing a martial arts instructor can think of is more difficult than the process of becoming a special forces soldier. Most services require potential trainees to pass through a hellish process known as "selection and assessment" before they can even attempt the nightmare of the qualification course. The selection and assessment phase includes hours upon hours of daily, backbreaking physical fitness training, sleep deprivation, and other methods designed to draw out the best and the worst of the soldier's will to endure, prevail, and survive.

By the time the special forces soldiers qualify in any of the military branch courses, whether Navy SEALs, Marine Force Recon, Army Rangers, Army

Unarmed Fighting

The special forces soldier is naturally strong-willed and ready to fight; martial arts will help him survive.

Special Forces, or whatever, they are completely familiar with their strong and weak points as human beings. Nothing a martial arts instructor can do in six weeks or less will significantly alter an already iron will to survive, but what he can do is offer specific ways to help ensure survival.

When a civilian joins a martial arts school, an instructor must often help him or her become comfortable with the notion of being physical, but physical prowess is the comfort blanket for special forces soldiers. The instructor who wants to teach elite troops must first understand that his task is to help an already high-powered weapon hit its target. The special forces soldier comes factory-equipped with guts, stamina, and willpower, so the instructor's task is to train all the components to achieve a single end: survival of a close encounter with an enemy.

CHOOSE YOUR WEAPONS, CHOOSE YOUR TARGETS

The primary weapon you can develop for a special forces soldier is his mind—his ability to think and react under pressure without panicking. Special forces troopers continually train with this goal in other situations. Your job while teaching them martial arts is to hone their ability to do so in a basically empty-hands fighting encounter.

Many instructors pay considerable lip service to training the student's mind, but then they get lost in the hundreds of techniques that must be taught. This approach to training will not work with special forces soldiers. By necessity they are results-oriented, not in terms of years, but weeks. Teaching them to think and react instinctively, especially while fighting unarmed, is the only way to accomplish this.

When I train special forces soldiers, my goal is to make them able to react instantly and instinctively to any attack with an unconscious counterattack, which means they must be able to react without thinking about which weapons to use or how to use them. To accomplish this, I first limit the possible choices they can consider, then endlessly drill these limited techniques into their brains and nervous systems until they become reflex actions. Then I put the soldiers into uncontrolled situations and environments and let them become comfortable with reacting to random situations.

Martial arts can offer a way to use just about any

part of the human body as a weapon for destroying an opponent. The challenge is to ingrain *a select few* of these choices into reliable weapons for the soldier being trained in a short period of time. An excellent way to accomplish this is to choose the weapons that can be used most naturally, which includes the fist, an open-handed slap, the hand to claw, the knees, the elbows, and certain natural kicks. Each of these techniques seems natural for a typical person to use. The next step then is to teach the soldier which weapon to use on what target. Again, this must be accomplished by showing only one or two ways to do it.

During the first week or so of training, the soldiers perform countless repetitions of weapon-to-target drills. One method is to have trainees face each other and then alternate counterattacking each other using a single technique such as a claw to the face—nothing more. They may move in circles, maneuver around obstacles, or roll around on the ground, but the only technique they can use is a claw to the face until it seems completely obvious and natural. Repeat this exercise using other techniques, such as elbows or knees to the body.

TEACHING KICKING TECHNIQUES

Whether a student has enrolled in a martial arts school or is being taught martial arts in special situations, kicking is absolutely the hardest weapon to develop. People are comfortable walking on two feet, but when one leaves the ground for something like kicking, alarms go off in the head and the body becomes unbalanced. But there is an almost natural exception.

Both children and adults learn certain kinds of kicks by playing with balls—footballs, soccer balls, kick balls—and with such a wide exposure to martial arts today, people can also be seen throwing their ver-

Train the soldier to kick as naturally as possible, which usually means low and fast.

sion of martial arts kicks when they're playing with their friends. These undisciplined and untrained kicks seem natural to them, and it is this same spirit that should be used to teach the soldier.

An excellent way to train them for leg techniques is what I call "natural kicking." Basically, I tell them to block a punch and then kick the opponent in the groin or knee. I offer them no specific way of doing it, which forces them to find the technique themselves— a method which encourages a much more natural reflexive weapon.

The rationale behind this training is to prevent the soldier from becoming too preoccupied with the one-two-three-four mentality of doing a proper front, side, or roundhouse kick. Most of the soldiers have tremendously strong legs from regular rucksack marching and swimming, so the natural kicks tend to have adequate power for stopping an attacker. You can spend time developing and teaching drills for kicking, but time is short for the special forces soldier, so the kicking drills shouldn't take up a disproportionate amount of time.

One excellent drill for the special forces trooper involves the use of a building that is to be cleared. Two or three opponents enter the building first and hide, and then the a team of special forces troopers enters the building to clear it. The opponents' task is to try to catch the clearers in tight, confined spaces where their weapons can't be brought to bear fast enough. The special forces troopers, if they are not using flash-bang grenades, almost always use some sort of natural kick when surprised. They kick the opponent away so that their primary weapon, a firearm, can be used.

SET COMBINATIONS:
THE BASIC COUNTERATTACK STRATEGY

The strategy I use when training special forces soldiers comes directly from kajukenbo training but is also found in other martial arts. The soldier is taught to block or parry and *at the same time* launch the first counterattack technique, trying to prevent the attacker from reacting by stunning or disabling him. Then the soldier moves directly to a takedown, finishing the attacker on the ground.

Each technique is actually a series that becomes a reflex. When the time comes to train the soldiers in counterattacking, they are never given a free choice of how to respond until the last two weeks of training. The rest of the course is spent developing a few simple counterattack combination series until the soldier can flow through each set without hesitation.

The secret is to keep the options to a minimum, which includes the number of series chosen to be taught. The special forces course I teach includes only ten combination series against empty-hand attacks, another five against kicks, ten against several common grab, pulling, or pushing situations, five against knives, and two against guns. All follow the same basic strategy of parry, stun, takedown, and finish.

One key for making this method work is to constantly instill in the soldier that once he launches his counterattack, he does not stop until the attacker is finished. In my course, when the soldier has his attacker on the ground, he is required to continue with *at least four* techniques, such as kicks to the head or ribs. Try to break the tendency for a soldier to throw one or two techniques then stand back to see if they worked. That method of fighting only works in the movies.

ADAPTABLE TECHNIQUE 1

Using Adaptable Technique 1, the defender evades and parries a round punch.

He grabs the attacker's arm, and while controlling the elbow, counters with a kick or knee to the stomach.

The defender immediately performs an arm lock take-down.

He finishes off the attacker by breaking his arm and dislocating his shoulder.

Using the same technique, the defender parries a stick attack.

He starts his counterattack with a kick while maintaining control of the stick.

He uses the same arm lock technique to smash the attacker to the ground.

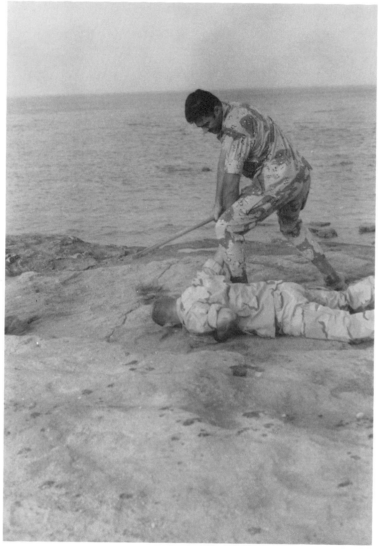

The defender then uses the stick to finish off the attacker.

ADAPTABLE TECHNIQUE 2

Using Adaptable Technique 2, the defender (left) evades and prepares to parry a straight punch.

The parry immediately becomes a choke out as the defender keeps moving behind the attacker.

*Keeping the attacker off balance, the defender keeps
choking him until the attacker is unconscious or dead.*

*The defender can also use Adaptable Technique 2
against a stick attack.*

This time he uses the stick as the choking weapon.

The stick, coupled with the knee, can also be used to break the attacker's neck.

ADAPTABLE TECHNIQUE 3

Using Adaptable Technique 3, the defender prepares to blend with the incoming straight punch.

He controls the attacker's arm and starts his counterattack.

The first counter is a hammerfist to the groin.

The defender then smoothly flows into an outside wrist lock and takedown.

After taking the opponent to the ground, he can finish with whatever techniques are necessary.

Using the same technique, the defender prepares to blend with a knife thrust attack.

Making sure he has control of the knife, the defender can then counter.

The defender counters with a hammerfist to the groin, still controlling the wrist and knife.

The defender uses an outside wrist lock and throw to take the attacker down.

Once the attacker is on the ground, the defender can use the knife to finish him off.

Unarmed Fighting

• • •

During the last two weeks of training, the fighting situations consist of series of unannounced and unpredictable situations where all a soldier can do is react. I have used several means to accomplish this, including a course similar to the law enforcement shooting town. A soldier walks through an informal, crudely constructed course where others are waiting behind obstacles to attack him. A variation is to send two soldiers through the hidden attack course together.

Please notice that these methods are designed for special forces soldiers who will be using the training in a combat environment where taking prisoners is not a priority. The methods would, of course, need to be adapted for other special situations, such as law enforcement SWAT teams and other similar units.

When choosing specific technique combinations to teach special forces soldiers, you should pay particular attention to how adaptable the technique series is. Why teach one series for empty-hand attacks and another for armed attacks if there is one that will work for both situations? Remember that the key to developing instant, uninhibited reflexes is to severely limit the counterattack options without sacrificing utility.

43

Ground Fighting

Sooner or later, most fights end up on the ground. The street fighter may be trying to beat you but not necessarily kill you. The special forces soldier, however, is functioning in a different context: Either he dies or the enemy dies. The elite soldier is not trying to take prisoners. There are, of course, exceptions to this, but for our purposes I will stay with the idea that the special forces soldier's situation is that his primary weapons have failed, e.g., he has run out of ammunition, or he is attempting to escape and evade.

Given these specifics, the special forces soldier has an advantage over someone learning martial arts in order to survive on the lawsuit-dominated city streets. He doesn't need to concern himself with intricate, precise maneuvers. He needs to win. He doesn't need to concern himself with whether he has used excessive force. For him, the right amount of force is that which allows him to survive.

When the skills of ground fighting are applied to this context, the special forces soldier's system of training can be much simpler. Ground fighting is an often neglected part of martial arts training in some specific styles. Other styles, the famous Gracie system of jujutsu most notably, have taken the art of ground fighting to new levels of skill and mastery, which by definition requires considerable training and practice.

I return to the same problem of training the special forces soldier: the constraints of time and the need for simplicity. One solution I use is a three-stage method for training elite troops in ground fighting.

STAGE ONE: FAMILIAR COMBAT

The first stage consists of simply making the men fight each other repeatedly with the intention of making clear certain principles, the most important of which is not to give up. Most soldiers feel comfortable roughhousing and wrestling, so during this stage you should force them to fight over and over until they uncover some of their strengths and weaknesses.

Most soldiers come to this sort of training with some minor skills, perhaps developed by wrestling in competition or just playing around in the schoolyard as kids. What this training eventually makes obvious is that most of the soldiers don't know how to end a fight beyond some sort of simple submission, or perhaps just physical exhaustion.

Find an area that provides room for ground fighting and close contact, but which is free of obstacles that could cause injuries. A sand pit is excellent. The following drills are helpful for stage one:

Two-Man Combat: Have two soldiers enter the combat area and fight each other for a specific period of time (for example, one 30-second round). Offer no rules or objectives—just tell them to fight each other.

Tag-Team Continuous: Pair the men off and tell one man from each pair to enter the pit and fight another soldier until he is tired. Then, when he can find an opening, he is to tag in his partner. Let the fight go on for several minutes. Again, offer no rules and no objectives.

Wave Attack: Put one soldier in the center of the sand pit and have the others surround him. One at a time, have each soldier attack him and fight him until told to change. Each soldier stays in the middle until he has fought all the others.

Combat Alley: Have the soldier walk through an area filled with obstacles, between which a few other soldiers are hiding, waiting to attack. Have the soldier fight against random, spontaneous attacks by the other soldiers.

Blind Battle: Much of the work the special forces soldier does takes place at night. A good way to simulate darkness is to use a simple blindfold. Have each soldier attacked while he is blindfolded in any of the scenarios described above. Better yet, have the men practice at night.

The soldiers will most likely fight even without any

clear objective of what they should do. Some will know how to use submissions, others will quit fighting when they grow tired or when the opponent does. Remember to offer no rules, insights, or objectives. After several days of this kind of combat, move on to stage two.

STAGE TWO: SPECIFIC TRAINING

During this stage of training, the soldier learns what the objective of his ground fighting is: to survive. This may seem like stating the obvious, but the soldier must learn that anytime an unarmed encounter enters the range of grappling, his sole purpose must be to disable and destroy his opponent and get away.

Keeping in mind the earlier argument that the soldier using hand-to-hand combat will most likely be physically tired, the elite trooper wants to avoid prolonged grappling at all costs. He must save his strength and continue his mission or his escape.

The main tendency that will appear during stage one training is that the soldier will perceive the fight to start when he and his opponent are making physical contact. He must therefore learn to see the openings that present themselves when someone is moving from close to grappling range. Instead of finding an entry point from which to take his opponent to the ground, the soldier should be taught disabling techniques.

For example, when the opponent has lowered himself into a wrestler's crouch and is rushing in, the soldier can counterattack with techniques such as eye gouges, cupping the ears, knees to the face, and elbows to the back of the head, spine, and base of the skull. He can then follow through with the techniques necessary to finish the attacker completely.

If the attacker and the soldier are already making physical contact, the strategy remains the same: Try to enter into disabling techniques. Nose smashes, eye

Ground Fighting

If the attack ends up on the ground, the defender should first try to relax and keep his wits.

gouges, strikes to the throat and the neck, and a whole range of other such devastating techniques can end a fight fast. The soldier must learn what the possibilities are and then learn to exploit them.

Another possibility when rolling around on the ground is a favorite of Hollywood movies: the expedient weapon. Finding a rock and hitting the opponent in the head or throwing sand in the opponent's eyes can turn the tide of a personal battle rather quickly.

During stage two, the soldier learns the possible weak points that may present themselves in a grappling/ground fighting situation, including the possi-

49

Instead of trying to grapple, he should go immediately for the vital areas such as the throat . . .

bilities presented by an attacker closing the gap. Some drills that are useful for stage two training are:

One Weapon, One Target: Choose one target and one weapon and continually drill one technique. For example, going for an eye gouge when someone rushes at you in a crouched posture.

Avoidance and Evasion: This exercise teaches soldiers how to avoid, evade, and outmaneuver an opponent's attack. For

50

. . . or the eyes.

example, one soldier attacks another using a single technique. During the first stage, the defending soldier avoids or evades his opponent's attack using only body movement. During the second stage, the defending soldier evades his opponent's attack, and then follows with a counterattack. The techniques used to evade the attacks are similar to those practiced in aikido and jujutsu.

Grounded: Start this drill by having one soldier dominate another soldier on the ground

Another excellent strategy while ground fighting is to use field-expedient weapons.

by sitting on his chest or sticking a knee in his back. In an actual fight, a soldier doesn't just magically find himself lying on his back with someone on top of him, but this drill requires good combinations of strength and technique to prevail.The soldiers must determine for themselves what works and what doesn't.

Whether you are the trainer or the learning special forces soldier, do not allow yourself to think of ground fighting as a separate moment or sphere of fighting. Ground fighting, knife fighting, and

52

In this case, the defender finds a rock near him . . .

unarmed combat are all the same for the special forces soldier: He is attacked and he must survive. An initial knife attack could easily end up on the ground.

(Please note that there are many martial arts instructors who are so knowledgeable about ground fighting that they could effectively train special forces soldiers using traditional techniques from their systems in a relatively short time. My basic argument remains that elite troops should be taught the more extreme versions of these techniques. A classical sitting armor, for example, can be turned into a shoulder dislocation or even an arm break with only slight addition-

. . . and uses it to smash the attacker's temple.

al pressure. This devastation is what should be empha-
sized since the soldier must learn to move in and out of
that technique fluidly, fighting on until the opponent is
finished. No soldier should be taught to assume that a
broken arm or dislocated shoulder will end a fight.)

Another important element of ground fighting
stressed in stage two is the application of choking and
strangulation techniques. If the goal is to take the
opponent out while ground fighting, then these methods have clear advantages and the openings for using
them often present themselves.

The difference in teaching these techniques to
special forces soldiers as compared to a traditional

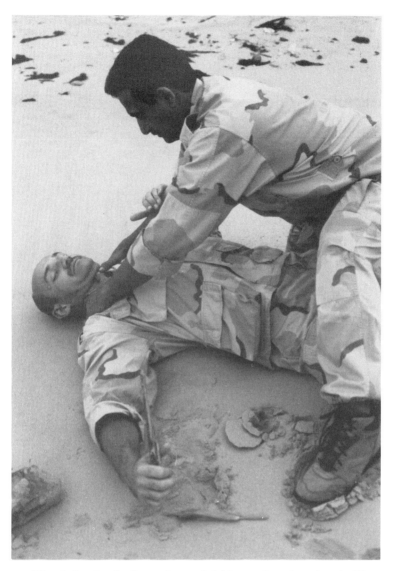

The defender feels a piece of driftwood and, using it like a knife . . .

. . . attempts to stab the attacker in the throat or the ear.

Three Crucial Groundfighting Strategies For Special Forces

1. Always try to attack easily accessible vital points and areas which will quickly neutralize the opponent, such as the eyes, nose, throat, and groin.

2. Try to use any field expedient weapons, such as hitting him with a rock, attacking his face or throat with a piece of stick, and rubbing dirt, sand or stones in his eyes.

3. Even more crucial than actual techniques is heart. A soldier can never be certain that a specific technique will work, but if he persists, if he tries to win at all costs, if he accepts that there are no rules in a survival situation and that anything goes, then the commando will have a crucial mental advantage.

martial arts student again rests in the time spent learning nuances. In many grappling-oriented styles, a student will literally spend years learning many different ways of entering into and then applying choking and strangling techniques. A soldier doesn't have that luxury, which is why the choices should be limited. Effective response equals narrowness of options and enhanced skill in their use.

STAGE THREE: BRING IT TOGETHER

During the final stage of training, the soldier returns to the drills and exercises found in stage one but applies the techniques, strategies, and tactics learned in stage two. The key in this stage is the repetition of a narrow range of responses and their fluid application in natural fight-like encounters.

Whether you are the soldier in training or the instructor, try to avoid the use of sheer strength and work harder on the application of technique. Once the techniques are learned, both speed and power can be increased.

Grab Counters

Techniques for countering grabs must address the context in which such an attack will happen. My previous contention remains that martial arts will most likely be used when all other primary weapons systems have failed, or the soldier is in an escape and evasion mode. A soldier in this situation will most likely face specific kinds of grabbing attacks, but before I examine them, I must first explain the meaning of "grabs" as used here.

Grabbing attacks in the special forces environment include grabbing and spinning into a sucker punch, chokes, strangles, bear hugs, headlocks, and other similar techniques. All of the techniques share one common characteristic: They are merely a means to an end, which in this realm is the enemy's attempt to capture, seriously injure, or kill the special forces soldier.

Grabs should be countered quickly with attacks to vital areas such as the throat.

The techniques for training a soldier to counter this broad spectrum of grabbing attacks use the same fighting strategies employed in the other unarmed situations. They are certainly worth repeating. The soldier is taught to block or parry and *at the same time* launch the first counterattack technique, trying to prevent the attacker from reacting by stunning or disabling him. Then the soldier directly moves to a takedown, finishing the attacker on the ground.

There are several methods for training the soldier for these kinds of attacks, but again the emphasis should be on keeping the responses simple. One

The defender is attacked from behind with a rear choke.

method is to place a soldier in the center of a sand pit and tell another soldier to attack him using a grab, first from behind and then from the side, without giving him a specific grab technique to use. This results in his making a more natural selection of which grab to use, which makes the attack more realistic. After several days of using this method, the many attack possibilities are narrowed down through the soldiers' choices to those that an attacker is most likely to use.

Countering grab attacks, especially as they are defined here, should include significant amounts of

As the defender turns, he raises his arm in the air . . .

training in an environment very similar to that in which the soldier will be operating. This could include the following drills:

Night Fight: This method has soldiers training in the actual darkness of night. Although this drill can be used for any kind of fighting, it is particularly useful for grab training. Try to use as many obstacles as possible. For example, train in a dark building or among trees where the only possible attacking technique is some sort of grab.

. . . and then wraps it around the attacker's arms, locking them. If done properly, this technique can dislocate the attacker's elbow.

Bus Stop: Another interesting way to train soldiers in close-quarters combat, especially for grabbing attacks, is to make them fight in strange, confined areas. For example, borrow a bus and force them to fight among the tight seats and in the narrow aisle. I have even used six-foot-diameter concrete conduits for training. The soldiers found it incredibly difficult to fight on a curved surface with little headroom.

The defender begins his counterattack with strikes to vital points, in this case a jab to the eyes. He can then continue with other techniques until the attacker is finished.

Firearm and Knife Defense

Training for defense against a firearm or knife creates a small dilemma for the special forces soldier. These techniques are the most difficult to perfect simply because they have the most dangerous, if not outright fatal, results if done incorrectly. They must be mastered, however, since the odds are very high that the special forces soldier will face someone with one or both weapons.

To make the situation worse, there is no other area in martial arts training where so many instructors teach ineffective and inappropriate techniques that, if used by the special forces soldier, will get him killed.

There are, in fact, very few methods for safely and effectively handling encounters with a firearm, especially from the front. These few basic methods are taught to American special operations and SWAT personnel, the German GSG-9, French GIGN, Israeli

Mossad, and British Special Air Service counterterrorists because they work.

Most martial arts techniques for fighting empty-handed against a knife were born, for the most part, in the land of fantasy. Overhead cross blocks and kicking the knife out of the attacker's hand are certain to result in the soldier's death because *they will not work*. Consider this recommendation from a book on classical jujutsu: ". . . quickly take off your shirt and use it to temporarily blind [your attacker.]" (I've left the title and author out because he is a highly respected instructor.) This certainly would not work for a person with load-bearing equipment on top of his uniform.

The point is that against firearms and knives, the techniques must be fast, effective, and, in keeping with the context of the special forces soldier, should end whenever possible with the weapon being used against the attacker to kill or disable him.

KNIFE DEFENSES

Every special forces soldier should be taught that in any confrontation against a knife, he will be cut and he will bleed. If by some miracle he doesn't, great. But the chances are extremely high that it will happen. Being cut and bleeding, however, doesn't mean that the commando is out of the fight. If this inevitable situation is accepted, then the soldier has an advantage.

Another advantage is the psychology of the person holding the knife. Most individuals holding a knife in their hand, fully intending to use it as a weapon, tend to rely on the knife at the exclusion of other techniques such as kicks or strikes.

From experience I can say that the debate about knife fighting can last all night. Highly trained and experienced combat professionals as well as street-smart knife fighters will argue that the knife is only one of the tools that a fighter can use. Others will say that there is virtually nothing you can do empty-handed against a seasoned knife fighter. They may be right.

My argument, however, is that a professional special forces soldier, given the full parameters of modern missions, is highly unlikely to meet such a master knife technician in his work. This might sound like nonsense to someone who thinks that the special forces professional regularly faces Soviet Spetsnatz soldiers or other enemies as highly trained as they are. Those who understand the adversaries faced by commandos today will attest to this simple fact.

The logical solution is for special forces soldiers to be trained to face two people. The first is an experienced, deadly knife fighter who most likely will kill the soldier in an unarmed situation, barring the miraculous intervention of a fellow soldier, a chance to run, or a lot of luck. The second is the *inexperienced* adversary who happens to have a knife in his hand.

Many martial arts experts, especially those who have experience in street fighting, say something like ". . . a real knife fighter will never use an overhead stab, or lead with the knife, or wave the knife back and forth in front of you before he attacks." They are probably right, but the special forces soldier will not be facing a street fighter. He will most likely face another soldier who happens to be wearing a knife on his belt but has little or no training in its use.

Techniques for defense against inexperienced knife fighters should incorporate the following strategic points:

1. The weapon hand must be controlled as soon as possible.
2. The attacker must be neutralized with a disabling or killing technique.
3. If possible, field-expedient weapons and

67

Against an amateur straight knife thrust, the defender slips to the outside and parries the attack.

diversions should be employed, such as kicking sand or throwing something in the attacker's face, or choking, striking, or poking him in vital target areas with a long piece of wood or pipe.

4. When possible, the attacker's weapon should always be used as the fastest means to neutralize him. The soldier doesn't need to worry about legalities, only survival.

Spartacus Knife Fighting

One method for teaching the soldier how quickly

The attacker's weapon hand is controlled . . .

a knife fight can turn serious is a variation of a training drill used in the movie *Spartacus*. (I even use the movie title as the drill's name.) In the movie, lethal body sword cuts were demonstrated and then practiced using a large paintbrush dipped in paint. Instead, this drill uses the largest magic marker you can find.

> **Level One**: Have one soldier attack another soldier using the magic marker as a knife and using it in many different ways, such as slashing and stabbing. Offer no techniques for defending against the "knife" in the

. . . and the weapon is used against the attacker.

beginning. Usually the defender will be covered with marks where a real knife would have cut him.

Level Two: After training the soldiers in knife-defense techniques, use the magic marker drill again. As time passes and their skills improve, the soldiers will have fewer marks, but remind them that *even one mark represents a cut.*

Against an amateur's slashing attack, the defender steps to the outside and parries the attack.

FIREARM DEFENSES

The series of photographs on pages 77 through 84 demonstrates a few techniques for properly defending against a firearm attack. These techniques can be incorporated into the drills described in the appendix.

I firmly believe that firearm disarming techniques cannot be learned from a book. Only an experienced instructor can show the soldier the nuances of handling such an attack. If he makes one mistake in a firearm defense, he will be injured severely, if not dead.

71

The defender then moves in while controlling the knife hand . . .

There are a few points that can be made about defending against a firearm, and these points should be kept in mind when practicing the techniques presented in this book.

1. When facing a weapon from the front, the only safe way to clear the weapon is to the outside. In other words, if the attacker is holding the weapon in his right hand, push his weapon hand to the right.

2. No one is fast enough to kick a firearm out

Firearm and Knife Defense

. . . and uses the knife against the attacker.

of someone's hand. The only kick that would work, using the theory of clearing the weapon to the outside, is an outside crescent kick. This technique is very slow and would be extremely hard to do in a military uniform and boots; *therefore, forget all kicking techniques against firearms.*

3. Firearm defenses should be used against real weapons only when strict safety measures are followed. *Both the attacker and the defender in practice should ensure that the weapon is empty. Check both the barrel and breech.*

73

Against an amateur's overhead stabbing attack . . .

4. A good test of any technique is to have the instructor use it against someone in the class. If the instructor, who in theory has been practicing the firearm defense for a long time, cannot do it consistently, then perhaps the technique doesn't work. Remember, when defending against a firearm you only get one chance.

5. When defending against firearms, fancy techniques have no place. Simplicity is the key. Beware of techniques that require you

74

. . . the defender slips to the outside, parrying the attack and controlling the arm . . .

to switch hands, turn under the attacker's arm, and so on.

6. Remember that in a real situation, when the attacker has a firearm and you decide to defend against it, he will not just stand there and watch you. Be very wary of techniques that require an extra second or two where the attacker just stands by as you defend. Can you do the techniques while both of you are in motion, or does the technique require him to be standing still when he pokes the weapon at you?

. . . then uses his leverage to drive the knife into the attacker's body.

7. Use common sense when learning weapon defenses. If it seems to you that the technique doesn't work, it probably doesn't. This is especially true when watching a potential instructor do the technique. If your life will depend on it, make sure it works.

Front firearm attacks should, without exception, be cleared to the outside. If the attacker holds the weapon in his right hand, then it should be pushed to the right.

The weapon is parried to the outside by a combination of the defender's body moving in the opposite direction and pushing the weapon away.

The weapon can then be controlled by flexing the attacker's wrist back into a lock.

Using the basic clearing method . . .

. . . the defender clears the weapon to the outside . . .

*. . . then, quickly bringing his left hand under the
weapon's muzzle . . .*

Firearm and Knife Defense

. . . the defender can force the weapon back into the attacker and attempt to fire it . . .

. . . or strip it away and fire.

Mental Training

The special forces soldier faces a fundamental paradox when learning martial arts techniques: How do you practice and master something the actual application of which results in the opponent's death? The answer has two parts. The soldier first must learn the actual physical skills involved, such as kicking, evasive movement, and the like. The second part, whether learning to be a military sniper or practicing martial arts, relies on mental training.

Professional and amateur athletes, especially in recent years, have learned to depend more on developing a complex set of mental skills, which includes improving concentration and focusing on the visualization of the performance environment, performance emotions, and perfection of technique. The special forces soldier can adopt the same training methods and alter them slightly for his specific ends.

Martial arts instructors, even when teaching soldiers, like to talk about serious-sounding things like intentionality, the flow of life force qi or chi, and other mystical, semireligious concepts. If an instructor tells his soldiers that "it takes a lifetime to learn to master the use of qi," how much confidence does he realistically expect the men to have in his training, which lasts only a few weeks? The solution, of course, is to remove this veil of mystical superiority from mental training. Professional athletes use the same basic methods, and most never approach any reference to Eastern religious thought.

What's most important when doing these exercises is not to alienate anyone by using language or references that may offend the soldiers or cause them to be skeptical. They are simply trying to learn how to relax and concentrate more strongly by using their ability to visualize certain images. Stay away from the temptation to make lengthy explanations about chi, or qi, and the host of other somewhat controversial martial arts concepts. You'd do far better to help them relax by making light of what you are doing: *"Use the force, Luke!"*

Special forces soldiers appreciate two aspects of any kind of training: first, that it is pragmatic and usable, and second, that its results are clearly apparent. There are ways to train soldiers so that they witness the benefits of mental training without having to wait a lifetime, especially when the reasons for and results of training are put into terms directly applicable to them.

MENTAL TRAINING EXERCISE #1: SIMPLE RELAXATION

Have the soldiers take a comfortable position, such as lying on their backs or sitting Indian-style.

Once they are comfortable, have each soldier run a mental inventory of himself. Starting at the top of their head and working down their body to their toes, have them tighten and then relax each body part in turn while taking deep breaths. For example:

Take a deep breath as you squint your eyes, then let the air out slowly as you relax the muscles around your eyes. (Work through every body part.)

MENTAL TRAINING EXERCISE #2: SIMPLE VISUALIZATION

Once each soldier is relaxed from using the exercises in Mental Training Exercise #1, add the following exercise:

Visualize yourself standing at the top of a large flight of stairs or entering an elevator on the top floor of a building that you have been in before. Then visualize walking down the stairs or, in the case of the elevator, watching the buttons light up as you descend past each floor. As you go down, your body relaxes more and more.

When you reach the bottom of the stairs or the ground floor in the elevator, imagine yourself standing in your favorite place: a real place that relaxes you in real life, such as a favorite lake or park. Visualize the place in as much detail as possible, seeing all the sights, hearing all the sounds, feeling a light breeze on your face, smelling all the smells.

After a few minutes, visualize yourself standing at the bottom of the stairs or climbing back into the elevator and beginning your

*ascent. As you go up, you feel more and more
relaxed and energized, as though you've finished a nice, refreshing nap. When you reach
the top, open your eyes. You should feel completely relaxed, energized, and invigorated.*

MENTAL TRAINING EXERCISE #3:
CONCRETE VISUALIZATION

I once wrote a letter to Col. James "Nick" Rowe, a
career special forces officer who survived five years as a
prisoner of war in Vietnam and authored a book about
his ordeal called *Five Years to Freedom.* (New York:
Ballantine Books, 1984.) (He was later tragically mur-
dered by guerrillas while serving in the Philippines.)
Colonel Rowe created the U.S. Army Special Forces
Survival, Evasion, Resistance, Escape (SERE) course
at Fort Bragg. In my letter, I asked if he knew of anyone
who had practiced martial arts in captivity as a means
of mental resistance against the enemy. His response,
through a third party, was that the prisoners were not
in good enough physical condition to do martial arts,
nor would they have been permitted to by the guards.

What Col. Rowe's book and other books written
by former POWs make clear, however, is the tremen-
dous importance of mental exercise to combat and
resist the enemy. Therefore, this exercise is designed
to accomplish two objectives. The first is to allow the
soldier to mentally practice martial arts techniques
that he may have to use someday, especially if he's
trying to escape and evade. The second is to bolster
the self-confidence and sense of mental resistance
against the enemy, specifically by practicing the
martial arts techniques on the captors in his mind.

Once the soldiers have achieved a state of mental
and physical relaxation by performing Mental Training
Exercises #1 and #2, use the following exercise:

Visualize yourself performing the personal combative techniques you have learned using an imaginary captor or one of your training instructors as your opponent. Visualize yourself defeating your opponent in detail.

Each time you practice, try to add more creative elements. For example, visualize yourself making use of field-expedient weapons like rocks and sticks. Try to watch (or imagine watching) your opponent carefully during your day-to-day encounters, looking for signs of his psychology and other elements that might give you clues about the way he would fight physically. Then incorporate this information into your mental training.

Most importantly, always see yourself defeating your opponent with more speed, more efficient techniques, and less use of brute force. Outthink him and then take him out.

MENTAL TRAINING EXERCISE #4:
SOLO TRAINING

This exercise is basically a repetition of Mental Training Exercise #3, but instead of beating imaginary captors or instructors, the soldier visualizes himself defeating the people with whom he fights on a daily basis during his training. They could be fellow members of his team or other members of a specific training course. The basic principles remain the same.

Appendix:
Training Methods
and Drills

T his appendix is a complete list of the various drills and training methods described in previous chapters. Use them as departure points to creating your own.

UNARMED FIGHTING TECHNIQUES

Natural Weapons
Martial arts can offer a way to use just about any part of the human body as a weapon for destroying an opponent. The challenge is to ingrain *a select few* of these into reliable weapons for the soldier being trained in a short period of time. Choose the weapons that can be used most naturally, including the fist, an open-handed slap, the hand to claw, the knees, the elbows, and certain natural kicks.

Single Weapons

Have each pair of soldiers face each other and then alternate counterattacking each other using a single technique such as a claw to the face—nothing more. They may move in circles, maneuver around obstacles, roll around on the ground, but the only technique they can use is a claw to the face until it seems completely obvious and natural. Repeat this exercise using other techniques, such as elbows or knees to the body.

Natural Kicking

With the soldiers still training in pairs, tell them to take turns blocking a punch and then kicking their opponent in the groin or knee. Offer them no specific way of doing it, thus forcing them to figure out the technique themselves—a method that encourages a much more natural reflexive weapon.

Flash Kicking

Have two or three opponents enter a building and hide. Then have a team of special forces troopers enter the building to clear it. The opponents' task is to try to catch the clearers in tight, confined spaces where their weapons can't be brought to bear fast enough. The special forces troopers, if they are not using flash-bang grenades, almost always use some sort of natural kick when surprised. They kick the opponent away so that their primary weapon, a firearm, can be used.

E & E Alley

During the last two weeks of training, the fighting situations consist of a series of unannounced and unpredictable situations where all a soldier can do is react. There are several means to accomplish this, including using a course similar to the law enforcement shooting town. A soldier walks through an informal, crudely constructed course where others are waiting behind obstacles to attack him. A variation is to send two soldiers through the hidden attack course together.

GROUND FIGHTING

Stage One: Familiar Combat

Grappling

Make the soldiers fight each other repeatedly with the intention of making clear certain principles, the most important of which is not to give up. Most soldiers feel comfortable rough-housing and wrestling, so force them to fight over and over until they uncover some of their strengths and weaknesses.

Bold Rush

With the soldiers in pairs, have each one take turns lowering himself into a wrestler's crouch and rushing at the other soldier, who can counterattack with techniques such as eye gouges, cupping the ears, knees to the face, and elbows to the back of the head, spine, and base of the skull, and then follow through with the techniques necessary to finish the attacker completely.

Two-Man Combat

Have two soldiers enter the combat area and fight each other for a specific period of time (for example, one 30-second round). Offer no rules or objectives—just tell them to fight each other.

Tag-Team Continuous

Pair the soldiers off and tell one man from each pair to enter a sand pit and fight another soldier until he is tired. Then, when he can find an opening, he is to tag in his partner. Let the fight go on for several minutes. Offer no rules and no objectives.

Wave Attack

Put one soldier in the center of the sand pit and have the others surround him. One at a time, have each soldier attack him and fight him until told to change. Each soldier stays in the middle until he has fought all the others.

Combat Alley

Have the soldier walk through an area filled with obstacles, between which a few other soldiers are hiding, waiting to attack. Have him fight against random, spontaneous attacks by the other soldiers.

Blind Battle

Because much of the special forces soldier's work takes place at night, a good way to simulate darkness is to use a simple blindfold. Have each soldier attacked while he is blindfolded using any of the training drills.

Stage Two: Specific Training

One Weapon, One Target

Choose one target and one weapon and continually drill a technique. For example, going for an eye gouge when someone rushes you in a crouched posture.

Avoidance and Evasion

These exercises teach the soldier how to avoid, evade, and outmaneuver his opponent's attack. Start with simple body movement, then later add a counterattack. The techniques could be similar to those practiced in aikido and jujutsu, for example.

Appendix: Training Methods and Drills

Grounded

Start this drill by having one soldier dominate another soldier on the ground by sitting on his chest or sticking a knee in his back. In an actual fight, a soldier doesn't just magically find himself lying on his back with someone on top of him, but this drill requires good combinations of strength and technique to prevail.

Stage Three: Bring it Together

Here the soldier returns to the drills and exercises found in stage one but applies the techniques, strategies, and tactics learned in stage two. The key is to practice a narrow range of responses and their fluid application in natural fight-like encounters.

GRAB COUNTERS

Anything Goes Grabbing

Place a soldier in the center of a sand pit (first with his back turned and then later to the side) and tell another soldier to attack him using a grab without giving him a specific grab technique to use. This results in his making a more natural selection of which grab to use, which makes the attack more realistic. After several days of using this method, the many attack possibilities are narrowed down through the soldiers' choices to those that an attacker is most likely to use.

Night Fight

This method has soldiers training in the actual darkness of night. Although this drill can be used for any kind of fighting, it is particularly useful for grab training. Try to use as many obstacles as possible. For example, train in a dark building or among trees where the only possible attacking technique is some sort of grab.

Bus Stop

Have the soldiers fight in strange, confined areas. For example, borrow a bus and force them to fight among the tight seats and in the narrow aisle. I have even used six-foot-diameter concrete conduits for training. The soldiers found it incredibly difficult to fight on a curved surface with little headroom.

KNIFE DEFENSE

Spartacus Knife Fighting

This method, which teaches the soldier how quickly a knife fight can turn serious, is a variation of a training drill used in the movie *Spartacus*. In the movie, lethal body sword cuts were demonstrated and then practiced using a large paintbrush dipped in paint. Instead, this drill uses the largest magic marker you can find.

Level One: Have one soldier attack another soldier using the magic marker as a knife and using it in many different ways, such as slashing and stabbing. Offer no techniques for defending against the "knife" in the beginning. Usually the defender will be covered with marks where a real knife would have cut him.

Level Two: After training the soldiers in knife-defense techniques, use the magic marker drill again. As time passes and their skills improve, the soldiers will have fewer marks.

MENTAL TRAINING

Mental Training Exercise #1:
Simple Relaxation

Have the soldiers take a comfortable position, such as lying on their backs or sitting Indian-style. Once they are comfortable, have each soldier run a mental inventory of himself. Starting at the top of their head and working down their body to their toes, have them tighten and then relax each body part in turn while taking deep breaths. For example:

> *Take a deep breath as you squint your eyes, then let the air out slowly as you relax the muscles around your eyes.* (Work through every body part.)

Mental Training Exercise #2:
Simple Visualization

Once the soldiers are relaxed from using the exercises in Mental Training Exercise #1, add the following exercise:

> *Visualize yourself standing at the top of a large flight of stairs or entering an elevator on the top floor of a building you have been in before. Then visualize walking down the stairs or, in the case of the elevator, watching the buttons light up as you descend past each floor. As you go down, your body relaxes more and more.*
>
> *When you reach the bottom of the stairs or the ground floor in the elevator, imagine yourself standing in your favorite place: a real place that relaxes you in real life, such as a favorite lake or park. Visualize the place in as much detail as possible, seeing all the sights, hear-*

97

*ing all the sounds, feeling a light breeze on
your face, smelling all the smells.*

*After a few minutes, visualize yourself
standing at the bottom of the stairs or climbing back into the elevator and beginning your
ascent. As you go up you feel more and more
relaxed and energized, as though you've finished a nice, refreshing nap. When you reach
the top, open your eyes. You should feel completely relaxed, energized, and invigorated.*

Mental Training Exercise #3:
Concrete Visualization

Once the soldiers have achieved a state of mental
and physical relaxation by performing Mental Training
Exercises #1 and #2, use the following exercise:

*Visualize yourself performing the personal
combative techniques you have learned using
an imaginary captor or one of your training
instructors as your opponent. Visualize yourself defeating your opponent in detail.*

*Each time you practice, try to add more
creative elements. For example, visualize
yourself making use of field-expedient
weapons like rocks and sticks. Try to watch
(or imagine watching) your opponent carefully
in your day-to-day encounters, looking for
signs of his psychology and other elements
that might give you clues about the way he
would fight physically. Then incorporate this
information into your mental training.*

*Most importantly, always imagine your-
self defeating your opponent with more
speed, more efficient techniques, and less use
of brute force. Outthink him and then take
him out.*

Mental Training Exercise #4:
Solo Training

This exercise is basically a repetition of Mental Training Exercise #3, but instead of beating imaginary captors or instructors, the soldier visualizes himself defeating the people with whom he fights on a daily basis during his training. They could be fellow members of his team or other members of a specific training course. The basic principles remain the same.

About the Author

William Beaver, a 5th dan black belt in kajukenbo under Bob Maschmeier and Joe Halbuna, currently lives in Kuwait where he operates a martial arts school and trains hand-to-hand combat instructors of the Kuwait Special Forces.

His students have included members of the Kuwait Ministry of Interior SWAT team, Kuwait Airways Sky Marshals, and members of the Amiri Guard VIP Protection Unit. He also frequently trains members of the American Special Forces who come to Kuwait on foreign internal defense missions.

From 1990 to 1992, William worked as the editor of *Karate/Kung Fu Illustrated* as well as associate editor for sister magazines *Black Belt* and *Martial Arts Training*.

He earned a master of arts degree in philosophy from Miami University and a bachelor of arts degree in philosophy from Ashland University, where he returned briefly as an adjunct professor teaching courses that included Applied Ethics: International Terrorism.

William received an honorary discharge as a sergeant in the U.S. Army after serving on both active and reserve duty from 1978 to 1986. He was assigned to units in field artillery, military police, and special forces.